16 Ecommerce Business Ideas (2023)

Profitable As you ever known

Sam Skinner

Tables of Contents

Chapter One

Introduction

Finding the ideal company idea—one that meshes with your day job, enables you to work from home, or capitalizes on a talent you already possess—is sometimes the most challenging aspect of establishing a business.

A flash of brilliance is not required to launch an internet business. These examples of internet businesses prove that you may earn money online by capitalizing on your current interests, hobbies, and talents.

What's best? Several e-commerce company concepts don't need any capital up front. Dropshipping, print-on-demand, and self-publishing are examples of business concepts that completely relieve you of inventory and fulfillment duties. You'll have more time to focus on your strengths as a result. develop and market.

This article offers 16 profitable e-commerce company ideas for business owners who are struggling with creativity.

16 lucrative online business concepts to consider

1. launch a dropshipping company
2. privately branded cosmetics
3. Sell your creations
4. create products
5. Subscription boxes for sale
6. Construct online classes
7. launch a clothes brand
8. Turn children's toys over
9. Sell on online stores
10. Selling books

11. selling your pictures

12. Produce natural goods

13. Offer NFTs.

14. repurpose smart home goods

15. Selling your services

16. Become a marketer for affiliates

Chapter Two

1. Establish a dropshipping company
With the help of the dropshipping business model, you may sell goods online without having to own or manage the actual facility where they are processed and kept. This implies that you may launch an online shop and offer a variety of goods without having to deal with inventory and fulfillment.

Dropshipping is a sure choice if you're searching for an ecommerce company concept that needs no beginning money.

Dropshipping is a form of order fulfillment that eliminates the need for inventory purchases, storage, and shipping. Working with a dropshipping vendor frees you from such duties, allowing you to purchase goods only after making a profit.

popular goods to dropship consist of;

caffeine-infused goods

Choose a dropshipping vendor that has the products you wish to sell to begin. DSers, Spocket, and DropCommerce, among other applications, interface with Shopify shops. A product you sell via your e-commerce website will instantly be sent to your supplier for delivery to the consumer.

How to advertise

1 - Establish trust by adding customer reviews, ratings, and testimonials to your site. ...

Run Facebook/TikTok ads according to your marketing objectives and spending limit.

Distribute social media videos to increase traffic and interaction.

4 - Use retargeting strategies to prevent losing prospective consumers

2. Private-label cosmetics

With the private labeling business concept, entrepreneurs collaborate with a manufacturer to create unique items. Make money by private labeling cosmetics, skin care, and other health and personal care products.

.

Max Beauty's founder, Hela Timothy Make contact with producers who currently produce the product you want to market if you want to launch a private label beauty company. Collaborate on a formula together, get samples to assess their quality, and read feedback from other business owners who have previously worked with them.

After you've located a manufacturer, set up your online shop, add product listings, and then begin promoting your new line of cosmetics to get more customers.

3. Market homemade products

Do you like creating handmade goods? By selling handcrafted goods via your own internet shop, you may turn your pastime into a lucrative side hustle and make extra cash.

Popular products to create and market include:

Jewelry\sCandles

Spa bombs

Pins made of enamel Woodworking tasks

By adding your handcrafted items to marketplaces, you may reach more prospective clients. For instance, Etsy caters to almost 90 million customers, many of whom utilize the online store to find handcrafted or customized things.

Bespoke items arc difficult to match since you might be the sole source (supplier) for them and they provide clients exactly what they want (demand).

4. Produce products

Do you have a social media following? Sell fan gear to monetize your fanbase, whether you're a singer, artist, or fashionista.

For a unique design, like your logo or motto, use a print-on-demand provider like Printful. Finally, upload the artwork to whatever your target market would be interested in purchasing—mugs, t-shirts, phone covers, etc.—and sell them online.

An artist uploads a unique design (a green dinosaur) to a basic t-shirt via the Printful website.

Entrepreneurs may upload unique designs to t-shirts with Printful.

Lacking the drive or time to establish yourself as an influencer? Take advantage of consumer familiarity with well-known brands.

Popular brands like Disney provide trademark licensing agreements so you may profit from unlicensed items including their logos, characters, and catchphrases. You may upload them to mugs, clothing, or home furnishings and then sell the products online.

Chapter three

5. Market subscription box services

If you want to generate recurring income, ecommerce subscriptions, which consumers will spend $38.2 billion on in 2023, are a product concept to think about. Customers will pay you each month (unless they unsubscribe) in return for a subscription box.

Choose a market where clients already prefer the subscription business model. They are listed by Statista as follows:

food, drink, and groceries
Products for personal care

household items

apparel Books, games, and toys

One company adopting this business strategy to generate online revenue is Fresh Patch. The store supplies grass areas for indoor pet potty breaks. Its creator, Andrew Feld, advises anyone who is considering launching a business to "try and discover something that is vital and has to be renewed." More than 80% of his company's revenues come from subscriptions.

6. Design online classes

According to projections, the market for online education will be valued at $300.3 million in 2028, growing at a compound annual growth rate of 23.6%. With an online course, you may attract the millions of clients who pay for high-quality education.

Stephen Light, co-owner and CEO of the mattress firm Nolah, claims that self-paced online courses are among the most profitable digital items to offer. "You simply need to choose a skill in which you have extensive expertise and promote yourself as an authority in the internet world.

"Many course developers are using social media sites like Facebook and Instagram to nurture inbound leads and introduce their digital goods. The sector for creating digital courses is anticipated to expand rapidly as remote or online work continues. Before the market gets unduly crowded, it is crucial to tailor your product today.

Create an online course around a subject you are an expert in to monetize your talent. There will undoubtedly be someone eager to improve their skills in everything you provide, from cooking to ceramics.

7. Launch a clothes brand

Get a portion of the $180.5 billion that US consumers spend on clothing and fashion each year by selling goods online.

Even while you could keep the profit margins high by making the clothing by hand, there other business models with a lower barrier to entry, such as:

purchasing clothing at a discount and reselling it at a higher price

Print-on-demand services, where you submit a unique design to a piece of clothing and the manufacturer prints, packages, and delivers it to your clients. One businessperson who adopted this ecommerce business concept and ran with it is Hela. She has a thriving clothing brand and counsels aspiring entrepreneurs to keep up with current trends: Take athletic wear. Despite the fact that I don't produce sports bras or tights, I would include the trend by wearing this sleek woven crop with tights.

Chapter four

8. Rotate kids' toys

Each year, $94.7 billion is spent worldwide by parents and other caregivers on toys for kids. Yet, flipping damaged, defective, or unwanted toys and selling them for a profit is a good starting business concept if you want to earn money quickly.

Finding unwanted children's toys

Visit garage sales
Consult your relatives and friends.
For "job lots" of used toys, search Facebook Marketplaces.

To revive the toys, hone your DIY abilities. Put them up for sale on your e-commerce website to attract parents shopping for new toys without paying full retail price.

9. Market your goods online
Customers have access to practically anything they may wish to purchase online thanks to marketplaces like Amazon. Because of this, 63% of consumers, who spend $367.19 billion annually, begin their shopping trips on Amazon.com.

Check out the bestsellers section on Amazon to see if you can take advantage of the enthusiasm that customers already have. You may be able to buy less expensive goods in bulk from a wholesaler and sell them on Amazon.

Aside from Amazon, other well-liked online stores to sell products on include:

Handshake
eBay
Marketplace bonanza on Facebook

Although marketplace selling provides you access to a consumer base that is prepared to make a buy, it also has drawbacks, most notably reduced profit margins. Also, there is a chance that a marketplace may remove your mini-store and drastically reduce sales.

By running an online shop in addition to your marketplace listings, you may reduce that risk. That way, even if anything terrible happens, you can still run your company.

10. Market books

The typical American spends $113.87 a year on reading, with around 65% of people having read at least one print book in the previous year.

Profit from your writing talent by creating and publishing your own book. Online book sales are made simple by publishing systems like Kindle Direct Publishing, Lulu, or Reedsy. There is no need to store a stack of unsold books at home since they print and send books at the point of sale.

Not a talented author? Alternative strategies for selling books include:

dropping off books
joining the affiliate program for already-written ebooks
establishing a bookshop in your neighborhood

11. Market your images
Photographer by passion? To get a little extra money on the side, grab your camera (a phone would suffice), take some pictures, and sell them online.

The following websites compensate you for each license or download of your image:

Alamy\shutterstock
Stocksy from iStockPhoto
Stock Adobe

Provide photographic services as a side business to wring more money out of your fledgling company. You may apply to become a Shopify Expert or list your photographic services on freelancing websites like Fiverr and Upwork. For these personalized picture sessions, you may often demand greater charges.

Chapter five

12. Produce natural goods
Consumers who are concerned about their health spend $32.09 billion annually on natural cosmetics and personal care items. Develop and market your own high-quality, all-natural items online, like:

items for organic skin care
snacks and meals made by plants
vitamins as well as essential oils

Due to greater consumer knowledge of their lifestyle choices, consumers are showing an increasing interest in natural and organic goods. To aid those leading natural and sustainable lifestyles, you may start selling natural items online.

13. Market NFTs

Unique digital files known as non-fungible tokens (NFTs) may be purchased and traded online. A single item has been reported to cost $6.2 million to be purchased by wealthy NFT aficionados. Even a little portion of that amount might launch a successful online store.

Make a digital asset that can be converted into an NFT, like:

Videos, Games, and Music

Open a digital wallet after selecting an NFT platform to sell on, such as OpenSea or Rarible (customers will buy your NFTs using cryptocurrency). Connect your digital wallet to your marketplace account, establish a price for the NFT, and open the bidding process for its purchase.

14. Refurbish items for smart homes

At least with regard to our technology, we are a hyperconnected country. In their homes, more than 87.7 million Americans have a smart speaker. All they have to do is mutter "Hello, Alexa," and they have access to every piece of knowledge they could possibly need right now.

Yet, smart home goods are pricey; not everyone has $100 or more to spend on brand-new technology.

Look for smart home items to repair if you need a side company concept. Discover outdated, damaged, or flawed copies of:

Bluetooth headphones
home surveillance systems
shrewd vacuums
fitness monitors
climate-controlling websites

... and use your DIY abilities to revive them. Put a higher price on them and sell them on your e-commerce site to make a profit.

15. Market your solutions
You don't necessarily have to offer solely products via an internet shop. Get money off of your abilities by offering them as a service, like:

Writing for hire Translation optimization for search engines Designing websites Photography individual training

Michael Keenan is a free-lance marketer who sells freelancing services online using his SEO expertise. In addition to my day work, I began ghostwriting for businesses, earning $20 each piece, the man claims. I went full-time and started earning six figures annually as I continued to hone my service offering and gain more expertise.

The most crucial thing to keep in mind when opening an online store is to choose a market that interests you. This will enable you to differentiate yourself from the competition and create a successful brand.

16. Become a marketer for affiliates

No marketable skill? You have no desire to produce your own goods. Ecommerce business models like affiliate marketing don't need either. It takes place when you work with a company to market their goods or services while being paid a commission on any sales you generate.

To increase traffic to the websites of your affiliate partners:

Increasing your social media following
Create a mailing list
Post product evaluations and how-to articles on your blog.
Create comparison pages.
Spend money on web advertising that focuses on the perfect client for your affiliate.

Diversifying your partner network within a certain area is essential for success as an affiliate marketer. For instance, if you're advertising pet items, work with companies that provide food, toys, and medicine. In this manner, if one company terminates its affiliate program or refuses to pay you a commission, you won't be left without any money.

Conclusion

In general, companies nowadays must always work to provide the next greatest thing that customers will want since they constantly want their goods and services to be better, quicker, and less expensive. Businesses in this age of emerging technology must adapt to the many new customer trends and wants since doing so will be essential to the survival and profitability of their organizations. With the development of technology, e-commerce is advancing and growing in significance for companies; it is something that should be used and put into practice.

The opportunities have grown exponentially since the advent of the Internet and e-commerce, for both clients and customers. expanding business prospects and technological improvements while giving consumers more choices. E-commerce does, however, have certain drawbacks, such as customer uncertainty, just like everything else, but nothing that can't be handled or avoided by wise decision-making and company procedures.

When launching an e-commerce firm, a number of aspects and variables need to be taken into account and chosen. Examples of this include various e-commerce models, marketing tactics, and a plethora of others. A company will succeed and be profitable in an e-commerce environment if the right procedures and techniques are used.